Hooves in the High Street

The Horses of Alfriston

by

Cheryl R Lutring

The moral right of the author has been asserted

Phreestyle Pholios
Alfriston, East Sussex BN26 5XE

cover: Adam and Heidi Cowley on Leo and Willy
in Alfriston High Street
cover photos: Jane A Green

ISBN 978-0-9569138-9-0

Typeset in Garamond 12pt

Printed in the UK

Proverbs and maxims:

"Wherever man has left his footprint in the long ascent from barbarism to civilization we will find the hoofprint of the horse beside it." John T Moore

"One can get in a car and see what man has made. One must get on a horse to see what God has made."   ~ Author Anon

A dog may be man's best friend…But the horse wrote history.

Do not underestimate a horse's pride, or he will dent yours.

Horses give us the wings we lack.

And God took a handful of southerly wind, blew His breath over it and created the horse." Bedouin saying

"…The horse gave us mastery." *Pam Brown* 1928

"To be loved by a horse, or by any animal, should fill us with awe – for we have not deserved it." *Marion C Garretty*, 1930

"A good rider can hear his horse speak to him.
A great rider can hear his horse whisper. But a bad rider won't hear his horse even if it screams at him!"

"Until one has loved an animal part of one's soul lays unawakened."
Anatole France, 1910

"Bread may feed my body, but my horse feeds my soul."
Bedouin proverb

Table of Contents

This book is dedicated to all horses wherever and whenever, but especially to the precious ones of my own, among them my first pony, Prince, and later here in Alfriston, Rare Visions, Gem, King's Ride, Visions Extra Texture and Visions Leading Hot Shot.

Horse ownership is demanding daily commitment, as well as a rewarding, developmental learning process; each individual of *equus caballus* I have been privileged to know has brought boundless adventure, turbulent emotions from tears to fears, pride and falls of all kinds, countless challenges, and immeasurable fun throughout my life.

I thank and remember them all with love and gratitude.

> There is nothing so good for the inside of a man as
> the outside of a horse.
> John Lubbock, "Recreation," *The Use of Life*, 1894

Introduction

Lest the village be presumed an equine backwater of no consequence, this book aims to highlight some of Alfriston's unique horse heritage.

Unfortunately, not every representative of this 'noblest of noble beasts' can be included, but all possible gates have been unlatched in the effort to seek out and record as many as possible from the butcher's vanner to the highflying racehorses and the more recent exclusive imports.

Before the combustion engine's domination, the horse was the foundation of life everywhere and these loyal and awesome creatures are no less deserving of their stories being recorded than the pubs and ghosts, smugglers, bells, butchers and bakers, brick-makers, and battalions of billeted soldiers.

However, though similar to other communities in such ways, Alfriston also has some unique elements in its equine history ...

"Look back at our struggle for freedom,
Trace our present day's strength to its source;
And you'll find that man's pathway to glory
Is strewn with the bones of a horse." *Anon*

The old Racecourse from Racestand Piece

There is certainly no shortage of written words about the long and fascinating history of Alfriston, a village just north of Seaford in East Sussex. Nestled nicely into the embrace of the South Downs, in 2013 Alfriston's latest accolade became "The Eastern Gateway of the South Downs National Park".

Look anywhere and much will be revealed about Alfriston's Cathedral of the Downs, or smugglers, or ancient inns such as the Star, the George, the Market Cross, or Waterloo Square and many of the centuries-old private residences and businesses throughout the length of the High Street. However, the casual seeker would find it a little more challenging to learn of another aspect of the history of this 'jewel in the crown' of East Sussex.

More's the pity, the annals of the passing years rarely reveal much about the magnificent Shire horses that ploughed the fields and pulled the harvesting equipment, brewer's drays, and general work wagons; little is written on the finer horses who spent their lives in the shafts of gentlemen's carriages; even less can be found about privately owned ladies' hacks, family hunters and children's ponies; so the racehorse appears to predominate.

Therefore, it is with the racehorse that we shall begin the story of equine Alfriston.

Though the exact route has been tilled and turned by time and the plough, there is no doubt that Alfriston had its own racecourse. Some conjecture that it was on the side of the Downs on the eastern slope of the range that goes to Firle, though this does seem unlikely. Others contend that it started in France Bottom, and somehow made its way to Bo Peep and then back along the ridge toward the village. If the wording of the Tithe records of 1842 can be relied upon then likely the areas known as Racecourse Piece and The Rails formed at least part of the course and its attendant gallops at that time. Certainly a stroll up there reveals long stretches that look very racecourse-ish. This map from 1900 depicts the Racecourse:

Indeed, it could be these or any combination of the stretches in question because at the time horse racing was quite different to today's version of the sport. No neat railings nor laundered surfaces, no short dashes of a few furlongs ... but instead four mile heats over unforgiving countryside marked, at best, with a few spaced-out shrubs on each side of the designated route. A contending horse had to run its heat, and then undertake the four miles again in other heats until a majority was achieved. So a winning horse might race twelve miles in an afternoon!

Notwithstanding the vanished course, we do have other evidence of its existence.

ALFRISTON RACES,

ARE altered to THURSDAY, the 13th of Oc-
TOBER; on account of the QUARTER SESSIONS, at
LEWES, being on the 7th Instant.

A SUBSCRIPTION PURSE of FIFTY POUNDS, free for any Horse, &c.——Four year olds, to carry 7st. 12lb. five year olds, 8st. 9lb. six year olds, 9st. and aged, 9st. 2lb. the best of three, four Mile Heats:——The Winner to be sold for 30 Guineas, if demanded, within a Quarter of an Hour after the Race; the Owner of the second Horse being first entitled, and if declined by him, the others in the Order they come in.

All Horses that Run for the above Plate, must be shewn and entered the Day before Running, at the GEORGE Inn, ALFRISTON, between the Hours of Four and Six o'Clock, to pay ONE GUINEA Entrance, or DOUBLE at the Post; and the Winning Horse to Subscribe 5l. towards the next Year's Races.

All Horses to be plated by a Subscribing Smith.

₀ To Start at Half past Three o'Clock.

THOMAS GEORGE WILLARD, Esq. } Stewards.
JAMES HURDIS, Esq.

A Handsome BRIDLE and SADDLE will be Run for at 11 o'Clock in the Morning, by any Horse, &c. that never won more than FIVE POUNDS at any one Time, to carry Catch Weight, Two Mile Heats.

N. B. There will be a good ORDINARY at the STAR and GEORGE Inns; and a BALL in the Evening.

It is particularly requested that no Person will bring Dogs with them on the Course.

Race notice of 1785

An 'Ordinary' is believed to have been a set menu dinner – here it seems that enough people were expected to warrant utilising the facilities of both the Star and the George Inn. What a pity the notice does not specify where the Ball was to be held. A hand-written card lodged amongst other papers in the East Sussex Record Office states:

Alfriston Races Apr 4 1842
1. Race of 10 Sovs^m .... 30 hurdles at even distances; horses to carry 12 stones and to be the property of gentlemen .... and to be rode by gentlemen. Start at 12 o'clock.
2. Race for a stake (amount fixed on before starting for the first) ... with 20 hurdles, under the same regulations as the first. The winner of the first race not allowed to start.
All disputes to be settled by the Stewards or who they have appointed.
All horses to be nominated on or before Easter Monday
to Mr Coofer [could be Cooley], Norton.

Newspaper reports reveal that, contrary to some assertions in tomes on racing history, Alfriston was holding races from at least 1785 to 1893 thereby being active for more than one hundred years. One of the last of the races of 1893, was won by a horse called Roman Oak who 'had a capital gallop on the flat'. Ridden by Lord Dangan and owned by Sir Humphrey de Trafford, Roman Oak was considered a strong Grand National contender over several years, and won many notable steeplechases before being sold to Germany.

In February 1840 the general press reported:
"A novell and extraordinary sporting match came off last Friday on Alfriston Race Course, between a mare belonging to Mr Walter Woodhams, and a horse the property of Mr Cave, to leap

forty hurdles placed forty yards apart, and the distance one mile. There was a large company present, and everything being ready, the determined riders mounted – Mr Sampson on the mare, Mr Monk on the horse [meaning in this context a stallion]. The mare led the first two leaps, when Mr Monk took up the running, passed his opponent, made play at a good pace, was never afterwards headed, and won very easily. Considering the number of leaps (which were only three hurdles wide) it is very remarkable that neither horse baulked any of the fences, nor was there a hurdle broken." See Appendix 1 for background of racing.

Reference to the Tithe Maps of 1843 reveals stretches of downland with names reflecting the old racecourse. For example 'Racecourse Piece' and 'Racestand Piece'. The latter appears to have been at the end of the section known as the Rails which comes up from the Alfriston/Seaford road on the scarp above France Bottom. If a racestand was there it also implies the location of the finishing post, which in turn means the races were started nearer to the Bo Peep area and were run back along the ridge towards the Rails. It is not hard to imagine the thundering of hooves coming over the brow and down the track towards the finish, and it certainly would have been a wonderful place to have a stand as it commands magnificent views – either across the downs to the Weald or over to the sea. May have been rather bitter on a cold blustery day though!

In the early days it was a customary practise for longer races to start off-course and end up on the course for the home stretch.

A racecourse rarely exists in isolation, particularly one sited on good downland turf, a surface ideal not only for the actual racing but for the training of racehorses too.

There are the long gallops up on the Downs, the valley floor gallops as at France Bottom, and probably good use was made of the tracks at the west side of the village – including Furlongs and Haven Road aka Cherry Track – as the roads were before the housing developments of the mid-1900s. Too short to be actual gallops the latter would have been useful for quiet exercise days and in times of bad weather when the gallops could have been inaccessible.

Therefore, Alfriston would have been an attractive place to set up a racing establishment.

Indeed, the racing industry in the second half of the 1800s was virtually the only thriving business in the dying and desolate village; work in stables and related businesses would put bread on the table for many a family. Income could be derived as jockeys, stable lads, cook and housekeeper to the stable staff, flint pickers on the gallops, hurdle and fence erectors and dismantlers, various supporting roles such as feed merchants, saddlers, clothing suppliers and tailors, cobblers and, of course, farriers; not to mention the daily benefit to the local grocery stores and public houses!

K nown in the wider racing industry as Alfriston Racing Stables, the Wingrove – for reasons lost in time – has been so named since it was built.

The site later occupied by the Alfriston Racing Stables originally consisted of tenements, cottages, a Malthouse and gardens. Previously owned by Charles Hillman, the property was put on the market on his death. The business premises remained unoccupied for a couple of decades until the entire property was purchased by Richard Porter in 1864. As some tenements were still occupied, he moved his family directly into the malthouse.

Thirty-nine-years of age, fair skinned, blue-eyed and generously whiskered Porter, the Scottish-born son of an iron founder, also bought land including Sloe Field at the other end of the village, and seemed set on building himself reputation and position as one of the landed gentry and a racehorse owner/breeder. With the thriving racing centre of Lewes only eight miles away, and the downland so perfect for training, Alfriston was a good choice. Moreover, permission was in place for the training of horses on the Downs and, indeed, a trainer from Newmarket, Henry Gatland, was already in the village, living next door at Somerset House, a tenement then consisting of three residences.

The implication here is that there were previously racing stables, or at least some facility to accommodate racehorses, in or near the village, but it has not been possible to ascertain where. However, in the infancy days of horseracing, it had not been unusual for a family's personal horses of quality to be brought out to race when appropriate. To ensure their fitness and aptitude, they would be trained by individuals with the relevant skills, such as an enthusiastic groom. As the sport grew in popularity, competitiveness and prize funds, a formal Rule Book was instituted and it started to become beneficial to utilise professional trainers to produce horses to an adequate standard. The first professional trainer on record is Robert Robson (1765-1835) who trained for Sir Ferdinand Poole in Lewes.

Intent on his mission, Porter invited an ex-trainer of considerable note, William King, to design his new stables.

King was from Yorkshire, the son of a trainer to the Earl of Scarborough at Sandbeck Park. Young William worked with his father until he was eighteen years old and then had a spell in Austria, before returning to become travelling head lad at the historic Whitewall Racing Stables in North Yorkshire. He always preferred the training aspects of horsemanship over riding and readily took to being the private trainer of Baron Rothschild, his winners including Orestes, King Tom, Hungerford and Mentmore Lass, to name a few.

He left Baron Rothschild in 1854, married and took up the landlordship of Doncaster's Turf Tavern — a famous hostelry among the racing fraternity — where he could offer stabling for eighty horses. However, he quickly found himself missing his old life, and after nine years was more than ready to respond to a call from Richard Porter to come to Alfriston to design his stables and be his trainer.

Here he again picked up the reins of his successful career. A write up in the general press headed "ALFRISTON" announced "Arrival of a racing stud: the arrival of the stud of R. Forster, Esq., from Lewes, on Thursday last, created quite a sensation here. The jockey boys attended by their head trainer, Mr King, rode through the streets to their stables and attracted a number of spectators. This certainly is a step in the right direction for us, and we are glad to see that our ancient town is to enjoy once more the prestige which is formally held under those great patrons of the turf, the late His Grace the Duke of Newcastle of Bishopstone House; Lord Egremont, Tetworth; Sir Ferdinand Poole; Sir H Blackman of Lewes; Sir Sampson Gideon, W Durand, T H Harben Esquires etc etc, who were supporters of our time. May the day not be far distant when we may boast of a winner of a Derby or a Leger."

King produced many winners including Haymaker and Challenge and the celebrated Dalby (bay colt owned by W G Bennett) who came out to win the coveted Chester Cup in both 1865 and 1866 – the first horse to achieve this back-to-back double. Resident jockey Samuel Hibberd piloted Dalby on both occasions. One of the many newspapers that covered Dalby's return home, reported that, "This is another lift up for the Alfriston Stables and to the assistants of this far-famed establishment. Dalby arrived home on Friday evening, and as trainer and lads went through the streets they were loudly cheered by the inhabitants who had waited the arrival of the train." That evening the whole village rejoiced at the victory to the light of a great bonfire in front of the Star Inn. Another stated that Dalby's owner and backers would have pocketed something like £40,000 and added that the second win of the Chester Cup was "another feather for the Alfriston stables and those connected with the racing establishment there".

Suffering from kidney disease, King had bouts of extreme illness and started to have fits, including one in the Jockeys &

Trainers Stand at Doncaster. Ultimately the fits increased and eventually, after a bad succession of them, he passed away at age 47 in 1868 in Alfriston. Obituaries for him say he was much respected on the turf where his genial manners gained him many friends.

By 1870 Porter had completed the construction of his seven-bedroom house he called Wingrove, which replaced a former building at the southern end of the stable complex, his family had moved in, and he listed himself as a trainer. Likely though the 'hands-on' trainer for the interim was actually Henry Gatland who had earlier moved away from his training life in Newmarket – the horse racing capital of the world – and resided a few doors along the High Street.

By 1871, Henry's relative, 25-year old James Gatland was listed as the professional trainer at Wingrove, living in Somerset House. His racing business employed twelve people, comprising a Head Lad in Training (Michael McCarnie), nine grooms, a professional jockey (Richardson Rowell) and a stud groom. Sampson Mordan, another resident jockey, had completed his apprenticeship with Dick Drewitt in Lewes. Mordan was an odd character who spoke with a lisp and always referred to himself in the third person.

During this period Porter also acquired the old redundant tannery/curriery at the other end of the Tye. Later dubbed The Gun Room, it is currently the 'Cellar Door' for Rathfinny Wine Estate with the Alfriston Heritage Centre on the mezzanine. Porter made this compact building suitable for stabling five horses – who doubtless benefited from the high level circulating air provided by the open cooling slats once used to dry off the hanging hides. He also had acquired Sloe Fields at the other end of the village – presumably initially for grazing – and is listed in the Census of 1871 as a landowner.

James Gatland had many successful National Hunt horses in his string and three jockeys listed as riding at the Royal meeting at Ascot were shown as residents of Alfriston: D Huggett, C Parkinson and H Warne.

One of Gatland's owners was, of course, Richard Porter, for whom he had charge of the aptly named 'Alfriston', placed at Lewes in 1878 jockeyed by Henry Constable (Champion Jockey 1873) and Hesper who was sold for 2,500 guineas to Mr Alex Baltazzi[1] in 1876. Hesper had been the first race horse of the popular benefactor of jockeys, Sir John Astley.

Porter also bred Thoroughbreds and one of his mares, Slumber, was written up as "being bred by Mr Richard Porter at the Alfriston Stud, and it was a mistake on his part ever to have sold her before she ran as a two-year-old."

In 1873 – the start of the Great Depression – the record shows a consignment of Porter's yearlings being auctioned at Tattersalls Sales in Brighton. They included Wide Awake (a sister to Slumber) who went for 120 guineas, Flint-Lock who sold for 270 guineas, and several other unnamed yearlings.

However, for Porter financial difficulties were always knocking and there was still a mortgage arrangement in place with Joseph Henry Scotts, a funder to whom he owed a great deal of money.

---

[1] Baltazzi was a Venetian-born aristocrat, lived in Turkey and owned the Hungarian-bred colt Kisbér who won the 1876 Epsom Derby.

Wingrove, showing the two large glass houses and neat gardens in 1880s

Scotts eventually ran out of patience and obliged Porter to give up the 100-year lease of Wingrove. At that point Porter also gave up his racing business and moved to Brighton to become a club proprietor.

Despite having purchased extra land from Deans Place in 1890, Scotts put up the property for auction in 1891. There were no takers.

Within a few weeks, James Gatland put in an offer of £1,625[2] which, after some negotiation, was accepted. While the legal necessities were in process Gatland rented the stabling for a nominal rent of 10 shillings. His overall purchase included the dwelling house, the malthouse, stabling and stalls for 36 horses with loft over, tenements, cottages, and a garden of 24 perches (607sq meters). Also included were a double coach-house, harness room, saddle room, sitting room and three bedrooms for men and boys.

Interestingly, according to the racing press, Gatland's family had earlier come over from Switzerland, settled in Seaford and the land they farmed was between that town and Alfriston. Perhaps this is why Henry Gatland (who was to die in 1897) had come to Alfriston from his training career in Newmarket.

At various times over the ensuing years of James Gatland's occupancy, other Wingrove loose boxes were taken by prolific winners on the flat such as Somnus, a bay colt, and a bay filly, Medora, by the local stallion Lord Clifden. His steeplechasers included 'very useful animals' such as Lady Villikins, Bloodstone, Partizan, Roman Oak, Ormiston, Bedouin, Hagiographer,

---

[2] Approximately £160,000 in today's money

Hagiographer on The Tye

Hurley, Degramont, Heath Cottage and the charmingly named Half-A-Dollar.

He also trained Bonnie Scotland who, ridden by local jockey George Butchers in a race at Plumpton, made a jumping error which almost tipped her jockey over her head. Nothing unusual in that, but in this incident the horse had slipped her bridle which was held simply by her closed mouth on the bit. George's professionalism triumphed and he pushed the mare through the pack to the front. Despite no visible means of steering, they won. That remarkable bridleless feat would cause a Stewards' Enquiry today and no doubt did then!

James Gatland in the porch at Wingrove – 1896

Left to right:
Ormiston, Hagiographer, Bedouin, Hurley, Degramont, Heath Cottage, Half-a-Dollar, pictured on the Tye with the yard of Wingrove behind them.
Taken in 1896

Note: the tall building to the right was part of the Wingrove complex, housing lads and horses

However, the star of the Wingrove show was Wild Man From Borneo who succeeded in fulfilling a dream for his owners – winning the prestigious Grand National![3] Wild Man was newly owned by the Widger family of Ireland. Purchased for £600 he won two races for them immediately, so in 1894 they thought him ready to try for the great Grand National. In the event he came in a very respectable third in extremely distinguished company, but jockey Joe Widger blamed himself for the placing, sensing the horse had a lot more in him. Joe is on record as saying "… this little horse will jump the country!"

Therefore, to improve his chances, they sent Wild Man for training to James Gatland at Alfriston. Joe and one of his brothers came with him and assisted in the training. Gatland had previous Grand National winner Father O'Flynn in his yard at the time and considered him a better horse than Wild Man.

It was a foggy day at Aintree for the 1895 Grand National and the going was very heavy. Other company in the line-up at the start included famous achievers such as Cathal, ridden by his Lewes trainer Harry Escott, former winners Father O'Flynn and Why Not, and the later-to-be-significant Manifesto. Wild Man started at 10/1 but the downland training gallops stood him in good stead, and he ran a strong race, to be produced by Joe at exactly the right moment to pass the winning post a length and a half in front of Cathal, who was followed by the remaining seventeen runners. Joe had achieved his lifetime ambition to win the great race. It must have been an incredibly proud moment

---

[3] The Grand National is a gruelling race of just over 4 miles and 30 tough fences that is the 'ultimate test of horse and rider'. Today it has a prize fund of £1million.

too for Gatland to lead Wild Man into the Winner's Enclosure for the presentation.

Wild Man From Borneo - Aintree Racecourse Museum

After his death Wild Man was preserved by a taxidermist, and his mounted head presided over press interviews in the Freebooter Room at Aintree, where he looked down in disdain for over a hundred years. Eventually, he started to show the ravages of time and in 2006 the head was removed to safe custody in the adjoining storage room. Wild Man was unwrapped especially for the photograph for this book.

But there was more to Mr Gatland than the racing record shows. He also owned the Star Inn and Somerset House and is listed as a brewer. In 1892 he advertised the charms of the Star in newspapers, where he emphasised 'good stabling' and 'Flys at Berwick Station'. He also seems to have been a man of taste, not only in the presentation of his horses and stables, but also with the décor of his house, which was described as containing "high class furniture in perfect condition, Axminster and Brussels carpets graced the floors, Chippendale chairs, oil paintings, and a writing desk with a revolving top, full sized pianoforte, and superior tableware."

At length the ailing James Gatland, whose relative George seems to have taken over the training for a short while, put up Wingrove for auction in June 1898 and retired from racing. The National Probate Calendar shows that he died later that year on 26th December 1898 leaving £322 to his widow, Emma (nee Harriett). He was buried in Alfriston churchyard 'where he could observe the school and was sheltered by yew shrubs'. His resting place has been obscured by time, but there is a clump of yew bushes against the church wall on the War Memorial Hall side. As the Hall used to be the school, it is likely Mr Gatland lies amid these bushes, where unfortunately the recumbent marker tablets are too eroded to read.

That Wingrove auction resulted in a consortium becoming the owners which included the colourful MP Horatio Bottomley, whose ambition was to race on an 'extensive scale'.

Therefore, the racing facility and Gatland's boots and spurs, so to speak, were taken over in 1899 by James Harry Batho, who would train in Alfriston for twenty-seven years.

Harry Batho in porch of Wingrove with terrier, Whisker

Batho had previously been the jockey for Horatio Bottomley, one of his mounts being the highly regarded Hawfinch, which had been purchased for 5,000 guineas[4] from the greatly respected John Porter (the inspiration behind the creation of Newbury Racecourse).

According to Batho's grandson, Richard Hayward, he came to Alfriston in quest of a residence suitable for Rose, his bride-to-be.

Perhaps the connection with Bottomley alerted him to the possibilities of Alfriston, and he took the lease of Wingrove and its accompanying 200 acres, including the area of the old racecourse, and the 'Gun Room' which housed five racehorses in stalls.

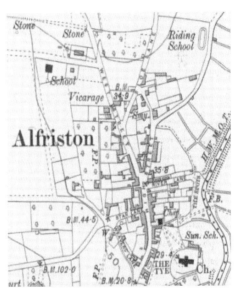

He also acquired Sloe Fields at the north end of the village, which had seven stables, a forge and an outdoor school[5].

He always asserted that one day he would build a house there ... and in the future he did.

---

[4] 5,000 guineas equates approximately to £525,000 today

[5] A 'school' in equestrian parlance is a dedicated area, covered or not, prepared to a suitable standard for the training of riding horses.

Among Batho's first patrons was Horatio Bottomley who put three horses in his charge, including the famous Hawfinch in 1898 who had to be prepared for the 2,000 Guineas, the Prince of Wales Stakes at Ascot and the Epsom Derby. But due to Bottomley's insistence that the horse show off his gallop to his owner nearly every week, Hawfinch had given his best before the Derby and consequently lost the race, costing Bottomley a great deal in his betting as well as the prize money.

Bottomley was, however, big enough to admit that it was his own fault and that he was totally ignorant of the techniques of producing racehorses. In his own words: "Despite the warnings of my trainer, I'm afraid that in racing phrasing I 'left the race at home.' I wanted to see a Derby trial every time I went to the training grounds with the result that on Derby Day itself the poor animal was more fit for the kennels than the race."

Good thing he had Harry Batho – pity he didn't leave him alone to get on with it!

However, another of his horses, Splendour, ran in the next race and won – Bottomley had placed £500 on him at six to one, so not all was lost that day!

He also owned Le Blizon a chestnut colt from France, purchased at auction for 1650 guineas. Le Blizon won many significant races including the Prix de la Manche in 1901, 1902 and 1903 and later stood at stud at Dicker Stud Farm for a fee of £7.7s to Thoroughbred mares.

Le Blizon

Another successful horse was Wargrave who won five races as a four-year old in 1902 including the Ebor Handicap, and the prestigious Cesarewitch in 1904. His win was recorded in a magnificent painting by the racing artist John Axel Beer (detail right below). Wargrave's racing plate, left below.

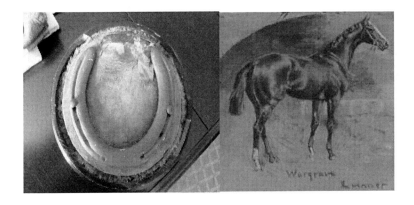

Amongst numerous others at the Alfriston Racing Stables were Bouton Rouge; Labrador; St Bernard; Northern Farmer for whom Bottomley had paid 2500 guineas and who went on to repay him by winning the Stewards Cup in 1899; Count Schomberg purchased for 5100 guineas in 1897 and his companion Berners; Gramcrip; Cobden; Sea Log; Sheerness; Faithful Don; Guadeloupe; John Bull; Pet Rose; Blairgowrie; the grey Butter Ball; Macmerry; Irish Fair; Vandal; Storm Witch; Minstrel Park; Longerline; Reprobate; Silver Salver; Santavon, Pickney, St Eyer, Benedictus; Promotor; Gentle Ida, the 1899 Grand National favourite but a faller.

Various jockeys had the rides of these horses over the period of their training, some apprenticed to Batho, some hired in specially to ride a specific horse in a specific race. For example, Le Blizon was ridden in 1899 by a young jockey named Dalton of whom it was said he was an excellent lad with much talent. Little Watts, a gifted young jockey from a racing family was specially engaged to ride Le Blizon in the Stewards Cup of 1902 but withdrew because of the terminal condition of his father. Others from the village would ride exercise from time to time including Edwin Norman and Mick Burgess.

In 1905 the Alfriston Racing Stables were put up for auction again and created quite a bidding frenzy. However, the hammer fell to Horatio Bottomley who then became the sole owner for the sum of £8,000. Harry Batho remained the trainer at the facility and the incumbent in the house known as Wingrove. The twin cellars of the Wingrove were utilised for storage of coal and the barrels of beer. The beer was for adding to the feed of the horses (a well-known pick-me-up, favoured incidentally by the great Arkle many years later!) and the head lad, Dad Cole, when preparing the horse's rations was known to help himself to a quiet pint as well.

Another notable runner produced by Harry Batho was the bay colt Long Set who, jockeyed by Billy Higgs[6], brought home to Alfriston the prize for the 1912 Lincolnshire Handicap. Batho celebrated this very prestigious win by purchasing a whole ox from Woods the Butchers and distributing joints to every household in the village.

The beef distribution on the Tye

Long Set is listed as belonging to Solomon Joel but often reported as being one of Bottomley's horses. Joel, English born, had gone out to South Africa in the 1880s to seek his fortune and made it in the diamond industry and railways.

---

[6] William 'Billy' Higgs, known as Farmer Higgs, was twice champion jockey in 1906 and 1907

In addition to the Lincoln, Long Set can claim the impressive distinction of winning three races in one week – located as far apart as Newmarket, Doncaster and Ayr! He was also the sire of good racehorses and in 1921 his son, Special Kit, also won the Stewards' Cup.

Long Set with Billy Higgs in saddle

Harry Batho was a prominent figure in the village and was a big supporter of local events and activities. With two friends he co-founded the Cuckmere Valley Cricket League. The silver cup he donated to this is still played for today. He was also an active supporter and funder of the Seaford Scouts, and devised and initiated the Alfriston Water Derby, located in and around the Brooks along the Cuckmere. This was supported by dignitaries from far and wide and provided hilarious entertainment for enthusiastic audiences. The current day River Race held as part of the Alfriston Festival week in August is an echo of this event. The contests were open to all local people and stable lads employed at local racing stables. The results for these annual events were reported in the press between 1907 and 1911.

One of the Water Derby's two-mile race winners, R Fletcher of the racing stables, was awarded The Wargrave Cup. Each race had a trophy for the winner and a donated worthwhile prize for them to keep, such as a diamond pin, gold and ruby pin, silver cigarette case, etc. The event attracted visitors and usually sixty competitors from far and wide, and local notables presented the prizes – including Lord Michelham and Horatio Bottomley. One hurdle race of over 220 yards and five flights offered the John Bull Cup which was obviously donated by Bottomley who founded the John Bull newspaper.

Another supporter of this event was a neighbouring trainer from Lewes. Harry Escott had undertaken his racing apprenticeship with James Gatland at Wingrove, before starting up independently in Lewes. A very successful trainer with Grand National and other major race winners in his string, Escott never lost his connection with Alfriston and was a friend and 'sparring partner' of Harry Batho. They would regularly pull stunts on one another, including one occasion when Batho was sent a haunch of venison from grateful connections in Scotland. By the time it arrived in Alfriston (no refrigerated vans in those days!) it was rather 'high'. He took one look and re-directed it marked 'with compliments' to Escott in Lewes – where the 'bouquet' must have gone before it! (For more information on the career of

Harry Escott please refer to my earlier book, *Lewes Racecourse|A Legacy Lost?*)

Batho engaged himself in the concerns of the residents of Alfriston and was generous to the children, paying for outings for them including trips to Cuckmere Haven in horse drawn wagons. He was 'the man to go to' for local residents finding themselves in difficulties. Neither did he fail in recognising the input of the local shepherds in keeping the gallops in good condition with the grazing of their flocks, and annually hosted an event for them at Wingrove's billiard room where they were entertained, fed and 'watered' and sent on their way with half a guinea each. They must have looked forward to that occasion. It was also traditional for there to be an Annual Dinner and Concert for the stable lads and their families at the Star Inn with sixty or more people enjoying the festivities.

It was customary for the travelling fairground to set up each year on the Tye. This annual event must have been made all the more magical by the generosity of Harry Batho who paid for all the rides for all the children for all the day.

○

The press was never stinting in its praise for Batho. A typical example from early 1922 is: "There has never been a better trainer of jumpers than Harry Batho, a fact which is amply proved by the records. St Bernard, which won for him at Lingfield, took the Three Mile 'Chase in a common canter and negotiated all the obstacles in the cleanest possible manner, and over three miles will take a lot of beating."

The reference to 'over three miles' indicates a contender for the Grand National. Against Batho's advice, St Bernard was entered in the National, on the insistence of the owner, Mrs Brownlee, but was unfortunate in that the horse ahead of him fell and brought him down too – a common hazard!

above: St Bernard on the Tye

left: Harry Batho with Mrs Brownlee, St Bernard's owner, at Lincoln Racecourse.

A necessary irritant in the life of a trainer is the often unannounced visits by the horse owners. Some were likely to visit on spec on Sunday mornings and would appreciate his prompt presence in the yard. For this reason, the Batho family changed their permanent pew[7] in the church to one closer to the door, thus aiding a speedy exit with minimum disruption to the congregation. Fortunately, it was only a short walk across the Tye to reach the stables.

The Tye also provided a good mustering point for the strings of horses as, in their carefully sorted working groups, instructions were issued about which gallops to go to, and each jockey was briefed as to the way to work his horse, and then they would move out onto the High Street and up to the gallops for their daily workout.

One of Batho's strings mustering on the Tye

---

[7] Florence Pagden in her *History of Alfriston* (1906) points out that St Andrew's seating was of the 'high horse-box pew' style – enclosed by wooden panelling with a lockable door – known as the 'true pew'.

A page from Batho's 'trials book' written in his own hand, recording performances over five trials in early 1898 for horses Hawfinch, Northern Farmer, Benedictus, Reprobate, Silver Salver and Splendour

Good for the village as the racing stables were, occasionally for some they were also the source of grief.

For example, Morgan the Seaford fishmonger, was also a bookie and would collect bets on his delivery round. For the 1912 Lincoln Handicap, Alfristonians wagered quite heavily on Long Set, perhaps not really in the belief that he could win so much as enthusiasm for a local entry. So when Long Set did win jubilation was the order of the day for the punters, but for Morgan it was a disaster – he lost everything.

Harry Batho had his own golf course on the top of the Downs to the west of the village. In the meadows just west of The Broadway he grew lucerne, a perennial grass from Mesopotamia ideal for making top class horse hay; and a little beyond that also planted the quick-growing sycamore trees as cover for his pheasants because he loved shooting. This copse still provides pheasant cover to this day.

Though not a Thoroughbred racehorse, a very valued member of the team would be the 'hack' used by the trainer to go up to the gallops and watch the horses work. The hack would need to be a steady type so the trainer could concentrate on his observations, rather than having to engage himself in controlling an exuberant horse. Harry Batho's horse of choice for this job was a grey cob called Joe with whom he formed a lifelong bond. Joe, though an inveterate jogger for any other rider, would walk quietly for Harry, as if he understood his job and took it seriously.

Once, as they hacked back home after a trip to Lewes, a thick fret descended on the Downs – as it still can do to this day (as has sometimes happened when I have been riding up there myself). Suddenly and unbidden Joe stopped and refused to move. Upon dismounting to investigate what was bothering the horse, Harry discovered they were right on the top edge of the very deep and steep Bo Peep chalk pit – another step by Joe and they would have toppled over, doubtless with fatal results for both. Their bond saved both their lives that day. Joe was rewarded with a home for the rest of his days, and was ultimately buried in the corner of the paddock, down near the road, at Wargrave.

Joe and Harry Batho; Snowflake with Harry's daughter, Evelyn, in Wingrove garden

Evelyn would ride her pony Snowflake everywhere, including to and from her school in Seaford.

Snowflake was very fast and keen, so one morning family and staff were shocked, horrified and distraught to find him dead in his stable. An autopsy was undertaken and it was discovered that the energetic pony had been functioning all his life on only one lung!

〇

Wars are never good news for anyone and certainly not for horses. Shocking numbers were lost in both World Wars, and local memory recalls that around two hundred of Alfriston's horses were requisitioned to go to the front and pull gun carriages. There is nothing on record to indicate that valuable racehorses were taken, possibly since, being a highly-strung breed, they would have been totally unsuitable for the horrific stresses of war.[8] Considered a 'morale booster', racing continued in restricted form throughout WW1, curtailed mainly by practicalities such as courses and gallops being turned to agriculture to produce food for the nation, unreliable railways, the requisitioning of motorised horse transport, and men being called up for military service.

However, horses of other types and even children's ponies were taken by the Remount Service throughout the country. So many conscripted, ultimately never to return, that in order to continue with the vital work on farms even circus elephants were put to the plough!

---

[8] See Appendix 2

Harry Batho was the first in Alfriston to learn that the war was over. No sooner had he taken the telephone call than Evelyn saddled up Pawnee, who had escaped conscription, and, as self-appointed mounted 'village cryer', cantered around the streets joyfully shouting "It's over, it's over". Thus Alfriston residents received the good news. However, this was the only time Evelyn broke the golden rule about never cantering a horse on a hard surface! Pawnee had been given to Evelyn by a family friend whose daughter had not been able to cope with his spirit. Registered in the Indian Stud Book, Pawnee was a polo pony and lived up to his inherent skills in every way, being sharp, agile and able to spin on a sixpence with ease.

Evelyn on Pawnee with dog Nick crossing the Tye (1923)

Of course, racehorse trainers do not do all the work themselves, but provide employment for many hands in the daily functioning of a stable yard. Sometimes this employment was casual and additional to the permanent staff – as detailed by Florence Pagden in her 1893 *History of Alfriston*, when a schoolgirl staying with the Pagden family had her hair cut by a local hairdresser who was also a groom at the racing stables! Well, it has to be said, one of the jobs of a groom is the pristine turnout of his charges and the care and dressing of manes and tails is a precise task calling for deft fingers and an eye for detail. A good groom is a valuable asset to any stable yard.

Interestingly, the 1901 Census lists two individuals who were "labourers on Race-course" – Edwin and Charlie Weekes. As actual racing on the Alfriston racecourse had finished in the 1890s, it is curious that this occupation should be shown so specifically – what were they doing?

It also reveals that, although resident in the High Street, virtually all the males in the local Pettitt family were employed at the racing stables in 1901, that is David and his sons, Charles and Sargeant (aged 12 – later to become a fly proprietor). Harry Lee worked at the stables too and boarded at 15 High Street. The boarding of lads and apprentice jockeys was a handy earner for local families that had space for another bed in their homes. In the Market Square several lads boarded with the bootmaker Jos Davies: twenty-year old Aaron Sandford, Richard Newman (24) and Henry Bird, aged 22.

At this time the tall building, referred to as the malt house or granary, provided accommodation for the core group of stable lads comprising Robert Charlton, Leonard Attwood, Bertram

Johnson, George Ticehurst, Gil Davis, Bertie Simpson, Louis Pettitt and George Robins plus two others. Fifteen-year-old groom Harry Parsons was accommodated in West Street.

The vital veterinary surgeon, John Miller, lived at Saffron Croft in 1901, with three racing stable grooms George Cole, Frederick Cole and Albert Ellis; next door was home to another groom Charles Hilton. With valuable racehorses in his care, Batho had the privilege of being able to call upon the Head Veterinary Surgeon at the Royal Veterinary College for any sick horse that needed specialist attention.

A snapshot of Batho's business in 1911 reveals he was employing a cook in the house (Mary Driscoll), housemaid Ada Turner, nursemaid Vida Page; and outside a groom for his carriage and working horses, Albert Pollinger, plus six stable lads/apprentices for the racehorses: Albert Glaiser, Alfred Every, Alfred Jones, Harry Sheather, Ross George Cole, Sydney Matlock and David Gordon.

Domestic staff lived on the top floor of the house. Mostly the stable lads lived in the tall building at the north end of the yard (now the Coach House Gallery, right) where there were dormitories and bedrooms on the top floor and later, at Evelyn's suggestion, a sitting room on the floor below.

above: south end of Wingrove yard in 1920s
below: similar angle in 2016

The north end of Wingrove stable yard in 1910s – Old Dad Cole nearest the camera. The boxes in the background were those of Pickney, Long Set and Santavon.

The north end of Wingrove stable yard in 2016

The north side of this floor housed a line of twelve stalls for racehorses, with access into the small courtyard at the front and on to the High Street. A sloping passage led down to the lower floor which is level with the Tye, where there were four stalls occupied in turn by the family horses including Snowflake, Jennie, Joe and Pawnee, Taffy and Dobbin.

The stable yard itself had twelve loose boxes – four of which were where the south end garages are today. Adjoining the house on the west side was Jarvie's box and next to that a box with padded walls that was used as a sand-pit – horses love to roll and this provided a safe surface and enclosure for them to enjoy themselves. Next was a passageway to the High Street, then four boxes and the saddlery in the north-west corner. Along the north side was a passage, then three boxes housing Pickney, Long Set and Santavon; then backing on to the Tye were the horse food kitchen (warm bran mashes being a regular requirement), engine house and battery house for electric lighting; apple store and boiler room. At first floor level there was a tack room and the hay lofts. The yard was closed off from the Tye by a high wall and a pair of large wooden doors, ensuring privacy and security. Nick, Harry's gun dog, had a kennel just behind the doors – for added security! In the centre of the open yard was a pigsty. This sty always had a walking stick leaning on the wall ready for the frequent visits of Lord Michelham, who liked to use it to scratch the backs of the pigs.

One of the apprentices of the Alfriston Racing Stables in Batho's time was Jimmy Hare, son of Bottomley's racing manager, who had a successful career in both flat and jump racing. He routinely took the reins of Le Blizon as he did for the

Royal Stakes at Epsom in 1904. His major wins included the Ebor Handicap in 1902 on Wargrave and 1911 on Pillo. His image was reproduced in Ogden's Collectable Cards set in the series called Owners, Racing Colours and Jockeys, in 1906. This card depicted him wearing the red, white and black colours of Horatio Bottomley. The 1911 Census shows Mrs Rose Hare living at 'Le Blizon House' in Alfriston which seems to have been adjacent to the house currently known as Hillside in West Street.

Jimmy Hare

Although Berwick Station is on record from 1846, many sources claim it is thanks to Bottomley and his equine interests that there continues to be a stop at Berwick. Known locally as 'Dicker Halt' it was a facility that would have been very convenient, not only for easier access to his activities in London, but this was the era when racehorses were travelled to distant courses via train. However, on one tragic occasion in 1899 the train carrying the five-year old Rigo, just returning home from winning the Stoke Steeplechase at Windsor, arrived at Berwick in the midst of a storm. Just as the horse carriage was decoupled from the train, a fierce wind caught it and hurled it into the siding, smashing it totally. Rigo was killed outright and his jockey who had travelled with him, David Read, was severely shaken and shocked. In 1901, David, it seems, lived in North Street with his wife, daughters and a servant. In 1902, Read was the jockey of Grand National winner Shannon Lass, owner Ambrose Gorham at Telscombe.

Also once when the train was stopped at Dicker Halt and the horse was being loaded, a train travelling on the other line blew its whistle. The horse panicked – as they will – and one leg went down the gap between the carriage and the platform and broke. He was put down on the spot. Chagrined at the trauma and waste, Bottomley immediately negotiated a covenant with the railway company that when a train was stationary at Dicker Halt, trains on the other line were also to come to a stop and keep their whistles silent so as to eliminate the fright hazard for the horses.

For obvious reasons Bottomley was also a keen supporter of the idea of a railway line from Polegate to Seaford via Alfriston; however, this proposal hit the buffers and came to an unceremonious halt.

At The Dicker, Bottomley not only built his vast rambling house, but created a large lake in the grounds, and on the land that is now known as Clifton Farm, developed his own racecourse complete with grandstand. The stable yard on the opposite side of the road to the house was home to his stud farm where he bred racehorses and stood his stallion, Wargrave, at stud.

One of Wargrave's progeny, Warlingham, was a big winner for his Swedish owner Mr Christianson, including the Cesarewitch in 1912 – an occasion that put £70,000 into Bottomley's pocket. Needless to say, the list of horses trained by Batho for various owners is virtually endless and there is no place here to credit them all. But some others he trained for Bottomley included winners such as Adansi, Bottor, Kilida, Pet Rose, Pollion, Sweet Mercy, The Gun, Grocer, Cripplegate, during the period 1905-7 and during 1911 Count Schomberg.

Adansi received a special notice of his own in the national press when he was retired in 1910: "Adansi, Mr Horatio Bottomley's wonderful old steeplechaser, has seen the last of a racecourse, his owner having pensioned off the old fellow in a comfortable paddock at Alfriston."

Though possibly a rogue in other ways, Bottomley does seem to have had an enormous fondness for his horses. Adansi, for example, was often entered in 'Selling Races' where the winner was up for sale to the highest bidder, and was often sold, but then immediately purchased back again by Bottomley, who said: "...this wonderful old fellow... he is one of the wonders of the racing world... he won me twenty races and at twelve years of age is still as fresh and lively as a two-year-old..."

He also laid one of his racehorses to rest in a grave adjacent to his private racecourse at his home The Dicker. As yet it has not been possible to discover whether this was Adansi or perhaps one of his stallions, or maybe Hawfinch.

Asked why horseracing appealed to the English, his response was: "because the sport is essentially British in its characteristics. Go to a race-meeting at any of the European capitals and you will find five out of every six jockeys are English lads. Foreign tariffs may prevent us from driving a bargain, but they can't stop us from riding a horse." He adds: "Try to imagine a King of England who didn't go racing. Why, there would be a Republic in a week!"

U

Harry Batho had long harboured the dream of building his own house and achieved this in 1915 with a house he named in honour of the high-earning Cesarewitch-winning racehorse, Wargrave. Located on Sloe Fields which he already owned, he created a smart gentleman's residence. The project suffered a false start because when the foundations had been dug the footprint of the house looked too small, so it was enlarged but retained the same design. The property consisted of eight bedrooms, four reception rooms (one used for billiards), and the usual utilities such as kitchen, scullery, boot room etc.

Ultimately all was ready and the family moved from the south end of the village to the north end.

Above: Wargrave as built and occupied by the Batho family

Wargrave – now extended and operating as Alfriston Court Care Home – 2016. The original house is clearly defined in the centre.

View of the Paddock View/Wargrave stable yard taken from the loft of the buildings that back on to Sloe Lane

The Sloe Lane aspect of Paddock View/Wargrave stables.
Still in situ in the gable under the apex of the roof is the winch
beam for lifting hay etc from a cart below to the loft.

The line of loose boxes in Batho's time at Wargrave/Paddock View.
Long Set occupied the fifth one down.

The Wargrave facilities lacked nothing. Batho added a new red brick range of stabling to the existing seven boxes, providing airy accommodation for the horses. In addition there were twelve stalls backing on to Sloe Lane with the lads' rooms and hay storage above. Running west-east a range of fourteen loose boxes, and on the other side another two boxes and two stalls next to the sand pit box. All in all, Wargrave provided very comfortable accommodation for family and horses alike. There was also a cottage for the gardener, and an on-site forge.

The usual feed rooms, garaging, engine house and battery house were on the north side and, on the south side, an acre of fruit and vegetable garden with peach trees and asparagus beds, all added to the complex, which had the benefit of adjoining paddocks, called Sloe Fields.

Much of the Wargrave facility remains though now with different functionality. The house, much extended, is a delightful care home with a large garden. The original seven boxes have been demolished but their brick flooring and brick pillars that supported the roof remain, nowadays utilised as a patio and

pergola (see left). The house to which this now belongs is a conversion of the original garage, engine room and battery room. Nearby another dwelling has been created from the small range of stabling that had housed Pawnee and Dobbin, and the blacksmith's shop.

The boxes with loft and lads' accommodation above which back on to Sloe Lane, known as 1, 2 and 3 Paddock View, is now three residences (above), which interestingly still have the original iron stanchions in place which hold up the beams on which the top floor rests. As can be seen in the picture on the right, the manger rings are still in place. I am reliably informed that the current suspended floor is two feet higher than the original brick paving stable floor underneath. Hence now the manger rings look a little low, but would have been at the correct height for the original floor. The line of boxes are pretty much as they were, complete with roof ventilators as can be seen above. It is not hard to imagine Long Set's head looking out from box 5.

In the 1960s stable lads in the bar at Lewes's racing tavern, the Pelham Arms, were overheard reflecting on the 'good old days'. One wag remarked "Then there was Harry Batho in Alfriston. He was a tough old b.....d and he had a daughter who was even worse!"

Tough and spirited she may have been, but Evelyn adored the racehorses and, despite the calls of many other non-equestrian talents, would happily spend her time in the stables or the saddle.

She was an excellent horsewoman whose skills were often borrowed by other trainers, particularly over in Jevington, who invited her to jockey their trial horses.

Of the horses in her father's training yard, Evelyn developed a particular fondness for King Sol, a chestnut colt, owned by Sir Hugo Cunliffe-Owen, a tobacco industrialist.

Evelyn would partner King Sol on training gallops and visit his stable every night to give him an apple.

Generally acknowledged as "a smashing sprinter" and "a class horse" King Sol achieved his place in racing annals with his decisive win in the 1919 Stewards' Cup at Goodwood, thus bringing further accolades home to Alfriston.

"To pilot a racehorse is to ride a half-ton catapult...
one of the most formidable feats in sport."
Charles Trigg, 1902 (jockey)

King Sol romping home leaving the field behind by a huge margin
in the Stewards Cup 1919 at Goodwood Racecourse,
jockeyed by W Baldings

A radiant Evelyn with her treasured King Sol in the Winner's
Enclosure after the Stewards' Cup at Goodwood 1919.
A glorious moment.

Five years after their move to Wargrave, the Wingrove came on
the market and the sixteen-year-old Evelyn's earlier prediction
that "we'll come back here one day" was vindicated. Her father
lost no time in purchasing the house with its adjoining stables
securing with it the precious gallops on the west side – France
Bottom and the area now known as Pleasant Rise.

In addition, he continued to lease Charleston Bottom in Friston Forest from the farmer, Mr Bray, and the gallop known as Norton from Viscount Gage. Norton ran along the ridge known as The Comp to Norton Top and on to what is now Bo Peep car park.

A winter Wingrove with one glasshouse removed and replaced by the Billiard Room to the right.

Batho added a substantial pitch-roof bedroom wing on to the east side of Wingrove, which filled the space between the line of boxes on the south end of the yard and up to the rear of the Billiard Room. The Billiard Room had been built for him earlier by Horatio Bottomley as a gift, in addition to the table and a host of racing pictures, it housed Evelyn's piano.

inside the Billiard Room

It was in the Billiard Room in 1925 that Batho suffered a huge stroke. Refusing to be moved, he remained there for a month before going on to the great racecourse in the sky. He was interred in Alfriston's St Andrew's Churchyard.

the grave of
Harry and Rose Batho
in St Andrew's front churchyard
overlooking the Tye

This changed everything for Evelyn. Her heart's desire had always been to become a trainer herself, but she was thwarted by the law at the time. Training licences were not approved for women until 1960 – an achievement of the gentle campaigning of Florence Nagel, whose licence was granted first and almost immediately the second was granted to Lewes trainer, Auriole Sinclair – but all too late for Evelyn. Although her voyage to Ceylon, where she was due to marry her fiancé, had been long booked, attending to a multitude of family affairs obliged her to postpone her plans in order to deal with the sale of Wingrove, clear up her father's estate and attend the needs of her mother. However, she would have the last word, so to speak … when the agent from the city came to view the land she obliged him to review the acreage on horseback – thereafter the poor fellow could not sit down for a week! The Batho humour at least, lived on!

So, essentially, with the death of Harry Batho, racing from Wingrove was over. In addition, Alfriston was increasingly becoming too crowded with motor vehicles whose drivers understood little about rural driving and negotiating strings of racehorses. The risks were perceived as too great, and Alfriston's appeal as a training centre began to lose its lustre.

☙

Others within the Alfriston clique of racing folk were also coming to the end of their particular courses: a 1927 newspaper obituary for 'Racehorse Owner Barnett Cohen', stated that "The best to carry his colours was Jarvie, who was trained for him by the late Harry Batho. Among the numerous races won by Jarvie

Jarvie

was the Victoria Cup at Hurst Park in 1924." For much of his time at the Alfriston Racing Stables, Jarvie resided in the first box against the house on the west side.

Having been ill for quite a while, Horatio Bottomley reached his personal finishing post on 25th May 1933 in hospital, eventually succumbing to 'cerebral thrombosis caused by arterio sclerosis'. The Dicker reverted to his ex-son-in-law, Jefferson Cohn, in settlement of debts. A clause in Bottomley's will required that his ashes be scattered on the gallops where the horses trained at Alfriston. However, due to the poverty-stricken situation of Peggy Primrose, his last stalwart female companion, nothing could be done for several years. Then at last in 1937, his nephew contacted the ailing Peggy Primrose, and together they travelled from London to carry out his last wish.

Pawnee and Evelyn; Taffy and Harry Batho

St Bernard and St Eyer

When Batho had moved his family and yard back to Wingrove, the Wargrave property was purchased by the infamous financier Clarence Hatry, whose activities, it is suggested, kick-started the great Wall Street Crash.

Epsom trainer, Percy Woodland, occupied the stabling. His jockeying career had been mostly in France but his major wins in the UK included the 1903 Grand National with Dumcree and the 1915 Grand National with Covertcoat. Covertcoat was unfortunately killed in a race at Punchestown in 1916 when he fell at a double bank and broke his neck – mercifully swift it is hoped! His hooves were made into inkstands.

Woodland started his jump-jockey career at 13 years old, and by 1903, at 21 years old, became the youngest ever Champion Jockey with 54 winners to his name. He was known for his very short-legged riding style and superb natural balance which led him to becoming the jump jockey to have the least falls on his record. Percy saw service in WW1 and was on his way to Gallipoli when he was injured, reported dead back in England, but actually taken prisoner of war in Palestine.

Percy Woodland

On his return to the UK he set up in training in Alfriston bringing fifteen horses with him to the Wargrave facility.

The record reveals him as a compassionate man when it came to the horses. Asked about the Bill going through Parliament to prohibit the docking[9] of horses' tails, he responded assertively, "It is a barbarous and useless and senseless custom, and of course it ought to be done away with".

Known as "a sportsman all over" when approached about a controversial winning decision in the Grand National which went in his favour but against Ernest Piggott, he remarked, "I have thought about this too. I know what I would be feeling if I were in Piggott's place."

He trained many winners but perhaps the most famous was Furious (owned by Hatry) who won the Lincoln Handicap in 1920 by three lengths. It was a lucky win for at least one punter who pocketed £15,000.

The Tatler
31st March 1920

detail from front page article about Furious winning the Lincoln Handicap with the austere but sentimental Herbert Robbins in the saddle. Percy Woodland leads Furious into the Winner's Enclosure

---

[9] Docking is the surgical shortening of the tail bone, not merely to the practise of trimming tail hair, of carriage and draft horses so the tail did not become trapped in the wheels of the vehicle, but it also became fashionable for ridden horses and racehorses.

Before the Lincoln Handicap, a journalist suggested that Furious and another four-year-old called White Heat should run a match race, with level weights, over two miles, for £500 a side, at one of the Metropolitan meetings, Hurst Park preferably. Percy Woodland 'who is nothing if not optimistic' answered "Furious, whenever and wherever he meets White Heat will show he is the better horse … he's a very game 'un." And so it proved to be. Yet further honours were brought home to the village.

We also know of Hatry's involvement with Alfriston from the family documentation of Ernest Reeder, a farrier who had emigrated to Canada to find his fortune. While there, he received a letter from Clarence Hatry inviting him to return to England, come to live in Alfriston and shoe his horses there. The offer was obviously too good to refuse, because he made his way back.

However, upon arriving in Alfriston he found that the job no longer existed and the house that went with it was occupied by someone else – this appears to be the original residence and forge in Sloe Lane, known now as the Old Forge and the Pony House. This happened in the 1920s and could well be an indicator that Hatry's fortunes had begun to change.

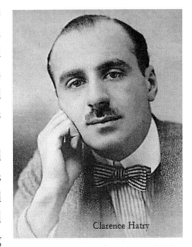

Clarence Hatry

Probably dismayed and disappointed, the family story goes that Ernest nevertheless gathered himself, his anvil and hammers and set himself up in a blacksmithing business shoeing cart horses, but this foundered relatively quickly, and he did no more than purchase an old army hut and began his own business in the chalk pit in Alfriston.

Hatry fell from his prominent heights, his banking empire crashed and he ended up serving nine years in jail for fraud. This presumably is what triggered Woodland's move from Alfriston to Cholderton where he continued his training activities. When he died in 1958 the racing columnist of *Sporting Times* wrote: "In his heyday, Percy Woodland, was the best steeplechase rider I had ever seen. In over a century no one has come near to matching his achievements…"

For a while the house Wargrave became a holiday let, and one family that used the premises in that way reported: "The house had an enormous range of horse-boxes, and Bottomley's Bottor had been trained on the downs above us. We filled four or five of these boxes, some with our dogs and their puppies, and two with horses, one for my sister and one for myself. … It was so heavenly on the downs, and every day we exercised ourselves and our horses…"

U

The record shows trainer Gilbert Bennett as residing at Wargrave in the late 1920s, which according to newspaper cuttings he was in the process of buying. When he started training in Alfriston his main jockey was the celebrated Frankie Wootton.

In 1926 the general press reported "Lord Glanely's flat racers, Grand Joy and Sunderland, have left Newmarket for G N Bennett's stables at Alfriston to be trained for racing under National Hunt Rules."

The Nottinghamshire Evening post in 1927 stated that Gordon Richards had been retained by the Alfriston Stables and thoroughly recommended that the safest plan was to support G Bennett's runner, Selected.

One of Gil Bennett's apprentices, Bob Turnell, is on record as saying that Gil "was a fine trainer, but a hard, hard man". Bob went on to become a very much liked trainer in his own right based in Marlborough. He died aged sixty-seven at his home.

In 1929 Bennett's owners had included Sir Henry Busby Bird who, though reducing his string following an accident at Hurst Park involving his horse Galloper King, retained two horses to put with Gil Bennett at Alfriston, one of these was named Treasurer.

Another owner to place horses with him was Lord Queenborough, of whom it was reported that his "colours were not so prominent as they used to be when Gil Bennett trained a string of jumpers for him".

Lord Queenborough was the father of the famous Dorothy Paget whose horses included the legendary Golden Miller, five times winner of the Cheltenham Gold Cup in the first part of the 1930s.

In 1931 Bennett had a brush with the authorities when he was summoned for failing to pay National Health Contributions for two of his stable hands, Stanley Noble and Edward Vaughan. He pleaded guilty but claimed it was because his business took him away from home so much that he had to leave the stamping of cards to his secretary. He had not realised that the cards had not been stamped. His costs were £10.10 and he was also ordered to pay a fine of £1 for each offence – a rather costly oversight.

Nevertheless, Bennett is described as the "most cheery of trainers" who in 1936 was tipped "likely to supply the danger to Mendicant Friar" in a forthcoming race. He is also noted in the racing press as bringing off a nice double at Folkestone with Zeni, owned by his daughter Inez, and his own horse Feud. His others were Crackerjack and Third Hazard.

He left Alfriston and moved to the Old Stud Farm stables at Polegate. This area is now housing, but several of the estate's roads have been named after famous race horses such as Brown Jack and Gainsborough.

The Wargrave house was converted by Mr & Mrs Denyer into a hotel and renamed White Lodge. Now it is greatly extended on each side and operates as Alfriston Court Care Home.

Meanwhile, having ceased as racing stables, Wingrove went through a series of names and functions. Initially it was run as a hotel by John Wilson, in World War II it was taken over by the Army (as was Star Lane Garage) and later operated as a pub named The Potters Wheel and then Chateau Anglais.

Its stables, once home to many worthy winners, became first tea rooms and then were converted into separate cottages for human occupation. Recently, Wingrove House itself has been refurbished as an elegant country hotel, and the adjoining cottages transformed into charming bedrooms with en suite facilities.

However, whereas racehorses are recorded in official documentation and newspaper reports, their hooves were not the only ones striking their ringing sound in the streets of Alfriston. Working horses of all sorts, on whom the functionality and pleasures of society depended, continued their daily unsung service to the population.

By 1909 maps reveal that the hitherto grazing paddocks that ran from the Star Lane/Weavers Lane corner, westward on the south side of King's Ride, now had a residence called White Court. On the six acres westward of White Court and adjacent to the Broadway there was a block of some eight loose boxes constructed around a well. These stables housed the riding horses of resident Colonel Crompton and his family, riding being a sport he and his daughter enjoyed.

The yard was demolished in the mid-20th century to make way for housing.

The well remains, located close to the road in front of No.2 King's Ride Cottages.

Slightly further west there is a brick building sufficient for just three horses and a building, utilised for cart horses and as an isolation yard by Wingrove racing stables. More recently the buildings were the base of a pig and chicken farmer. They remain there today, along with a relatively modern Dutch barn.

U

Carriage/fly proprietors plied their trade, for which there seems to have been no shortage in the village: Sarge Pettitt, Charles Norman, Jesse Potter, Henry Peirce and Joseph Dumbrell of the George Inn, were fly[10] proprietors. Henry Peirce resided at Cross House in Market Square with his family and staff, plus one boarder who worked as a stableman at the racing stables, Leonard Charles Jones, 28, from Fulham. There was a regular several times daily service to Berwick Station. Interestingly, it was Joseph Dumbrell who had the first motor taxi in the village.

Joseph Dumbrell (in front of the Assembly Rooms behind the Star)

---

[10] A fly was a light one-horse covered carriage, usually for several passengers, for hire

Sarge Pettitt – taken at the back of The George

It was a delight for me during my researches to find the postcard depicted overleaf. Just three years after Florence Pagden published the third edition of her *History of Alfriston*, the card was posted in September 1909 from Alfriston to Miss Pagden in Portsmouth. The message reads: "Dear Fanny, ….. this is Jesse with Betty, she will be pulling the trap when we meet you at Seaford..." For special occasions, Potter also utilised a stylish brougham.

At this time Jesse Potter, then 35, was listed as a jobmaster[11] and one of the local transport proprietors, who seems to have resided in part of Cross House in Market Square.

---

[11] A jobmaster was the keeper of a livery stable who rented out horses and carriages by the week or month.

Jesse Potter with Betty (roof of Wingrove in the background) 1909

Jennie with her governess cart

Racing families, likewise, had their own carriage and pleasure horses. For years an excellent driving pony called Jennie took the Batho family hither and thither. She was fast and keen and could put the miles behind her with ease. Unfortunately, one day, driven by someone lacking the skills for such a pony, she became unbalanced, stumbled and fell, breaking her knees. Sadly, she had to be put down.

Farm horses too, carried on their sterling work hauling wagons, ploughs, harrows, reaping machines – all the functions required to manage the land and bring home the harvest to feed the people. There were at least four of these majestic animals at any one time to whom Bank House Farm (off Market Square) was home. There were also several recorded as being at Rathfinny Farm, as detailed in a newspaper article re charges of animal cruelty – see page 79.

The motorised tractor nearly caused the extinction of these loyal workers, but certain breed devotees retained vital individuals and thus saved the heavy horses for posterity. Now, though some small farms, foresters and institutions such as the Wealden Open Air Museum, use them in preference to soil-damaging tractors, they are mostly engaged in the show rings and plough matches.

They can also be seen in some regions harnessed to the brewers' drays, delivering the ale to pubs and hotels, creating a tourist attraction far superior to the noise and fumes of a delivery lorry. Harvey's Brewery in Lewes is a fine example.

Harvey's Brewery Dray with shire horses Jim and Guiness

For a while though horses had the last neigh, so to speak, as the new-fangled motor vehicles would overheat and founder when tackling High & Over on the Seaford Road. On such occasions horse teams were brought out to tow the stricken vehicle to the top.

Behind the Star car park could be found Alfriston Motors which served petrol and provided servicing for motor vehicles of all kinds. This began when horses were still in use too and continued in the hands of the Lower family until 2015. Before that the barn was the base of Pettitt & Sons, village builders. Now it is being converted into residences.

The barn in Star Lane when in use by Pettitt & Sons, builders.
Their horse drawn work wagon stands outside.

The traders and artisans whose incomes were either dependent upon, or were nicely supplemented by, the use of horses in whatever capacity, included harness makers and saddlers, one being William Kidd who also owned land, another was William Marchant who lived in the Manor House but had his shop opposite in a building called "Saddlers" which has since been a café and is now Music Memorabilia. Also based there were Oliver Bristow and his sons Charles and William (15 years old in 1901 – presumably the same 'Billie' Bristow of later 'sweet violets' fame); and the breeches maker Cornelius Gibson who lived and worked at the cottage in North Street known now as Badgers (once The Urn).

Various blacksmiths and farriers worked from at least two forges in the village. The one previously mentioned at The Old Forge in Sloe Lane (built 1490), seems to have been the workplace of George Brooks in 1901. It finally closed as a forge in the 1930s when the last blacksmith was Henry Woolgar. In the 1980s the forge section was converted to a local museum by Geoffrey and Sandy Hernu.

above: The Old Forge, Sloe Lane, 2016

Inside the Old Forge in its Museum days – reconstructed brick-built furnace in the centre

Another forge was sited further down North Street and was occupied by Edmund Clive. Yet another was located opposite the car park entrance in West Street, which is now a small housing development known as The Forge. Here Les Edwards applied his biceps to hammer and anvil until the building and its attached orchard were required for development in the 1990s. It is now a rather charming enclave of stylish cottages with a clock arch, emulating a stable yard entrance, but best of all its working past is honoured by a wall of the forge being left in situ upon which is a wrought iron commemoration:

Blacksmithing involved a number of skills – making horse shoes was one, but they also made all manner of iron accoutrements such as gates, hinges, bolts, fixings for carriages etc. Farriery relates to the actual art of preparing the horse's hooves and applying the shoes correctly – a tricky and precise skill upon which the health and usability of the horse depended – as the old saying goes "no foot, no 'orse".

Unlike this day and age of travelling farriers, the horse requiring shoeing then was obliged to go to the forge. This was partly because most shoeing was done with hot shoes so the fit would be better and hence had to be applied near the furnace.

Of course, the local inns also had stabling for the horses of their guests, together with staff to take care of them. The Star Inn had the barns at the back – which operated in turn as barns, school room, and function room for dances – long since demolished. What is now the dining room sports the original oak posts and beams of the stables. In 1901 the ostler[12] at the Star was Robert Chatfield (58 years old) and his job would have been to attend to visiting horses: unharness/unsaddle, rub them down if they were over-heated, put them in a stall or loose box that was nicely bedded with comfortable straw, feed and water them. Having ensured they were comfortable for the night, he would clean their tack and then he could retire, but would have to be on duty again early in the morning to again feed and water the horses, and groom the bedding stains from their coats, comb straw from their manes and tails, pick out bedding from their hooves, and, when required, saddle or harness them ready for their day's work or journey.

The George was a coaching inn with stabling and horse care facilities at the back. Its arched access for the horses and carriages to reach the stables has long since been bricked in and now that area is the dining room!

ᴜᴜᴜ

---

[12] A horseman/groom employed by an inn to look after the guests' horses.

Snippets from over the stable door

In 1950, newspapers throughout the country reported that: David Dale had stables at Alfriston, Sussex, and had earned a great reputation as a 'horse doctor'. Horses which had broken down badly were often sent to him. Dale nursed them back to fitness and they went on to win races. The snag with this was that Dale seldom received a horse which had not broken down. His stable, in fact, became an equine infirmary. Nevertheless, he trained Brave Mic, a multi-race winner who insisted on the constant company of his friend, a goat.

Unfortunately, it has not been possible to find where Dale's stables were in Alfriston, though there is reference to him having stables at Bishopstone during part of the 1920s. However, he did move into farming, and ultimately, in 1947, at age 70, emigrated to Kenya and started a new career! (More in Appendix 7)

○

Newspaper reports of 1864 describe the 'accidental death' of Mathew Henry Vinal, who fell from the loft in the coach house at the Star. He had obviously been sleeping there when the support holding the loft up broke and deposited the stored grain onto the floor below, taking Matthew with it. Two carts were broken to pieces, one belonging to the saddler, Mrs Ann Marchant, and 'Mr Erry's horse was almost buried under the broken timber and oats, but fortunately was not hurt'. Matthew, however, was covered four feet deep in loose oats. Alfriston's policeman, William Richardson, was prompt on the scene; and the Star landlord, James Page, reported that the deceased had charge of a horse kept in the adjoining stable but had no leave to sleep in the loft.

〇

Report in the November 1899 Sussex Advertiser:

"A butcher fined for drunkenness – At the Hailsham Petty Sessions on Wednesday [in November 1899], before Dr G A Jeffery (in the chair), W Strickland, Esq., WA Haviland Esq., and J Gorringe Esq., Charles Humes, butcher of Polegate, was summoned for being drunk whilst in charge of a horse and cart at Alfriston on October 11th. Mr Lawson Lewis defended, and at his application all witnesses were ordered out of course. Joseph Christmas, living in high Street, Alfriston, said on the 11th October, between eight and nine o'clock in the evening, he was standing at his front door when he saw the defendant driving a pony and trap down the High Street at a rate of about eight or ten miles per hour. When he got at the bottom of the street he turned round and drove up again. He kept on driving up and down for about an hour. Defendant was drunk. Clerk asked "how do you know he was drunk?" Witness: "He was thrashing the pony so mercifully (laughter), and driving so fast". Clerk: "Mercifully?" Witness: "Unmercifully ... he tried to stand up in the cart but fell back on to the seat." Mr Lewis: "I suppose you thought he was very cruel to the horse?" Witness: "Yes". Mr Lewis: "Why did you not stop him?" Witness: "There was such a crowd. They were running up and down the street trying to keep up with him". Mr Lewis: "Why did they not stop him? Did he drive through the crowd?" Witness: "They did not stop him, they cleared out of the way whilst he passed them". Mr Lewis: "Are you in charge of the village in the absence of the police?" Witness: "I wish I was, I should have had him locked up". Mr Lewis: "Have you heard that Mr

Humes' harness was thrown about the road by a gang of Alfriston roughs and the pony turned loose?" Witness: "I didn't hear of that." In reply to further questions the witness said he had heard that the defendant had to walk to Berwick because he could not find his pony. Albert Muddle, labourer, of Alfriston, said on the evening of the day in question he saw the defendant drive up and down the street. He was drunk. Witness helped to take the pony out. The harness was put into the cart and not scattered about the road. Mr Pettit, builder, of Alfriston, ordered the pony to be taken out. In reply to Mr Lewis, witness said the crowd was not the cause of the whole 'demonstration'. They were perfectly quiet. Mr Lewis: Had your presence an effect upon them, then? Witness: Yes, sir. In reply to further questions witness said defendant sat down on the steps of the Star Hotel for about half-an-hour. Mr Lewis: Any signs of his being drunk? Witness: He leaned against the hotel. Mr Lewis: And I suppose every man who leans against an hotel is drunk. (laughter) Witness also stated that defendant was not helped into the trap. He was shewed the way in by a boy named Norman. He was not aware that defendant had made a complaint to the police about being 'set upon' by a gang of Alfriston roughs. Ernest Norman, living in High Street, Alfriston, also gave evidence as to the defendant's condition, and added that he did not go to the police station and make a complaint but sat outside on the steps all the time. Mr Lewis submitted that he had no case to answer. He suggested that a more impudent prosecution never took place. It was unsupported by the police, and there was no evidence at all as to the drunkenness. The Bench decided that there was a case to answer. Mr Park, of Croft House, Alfriston, said on the night of the 11th ult. The defendant came to his house and made a complaint to him. He went back to the village with the defendant and saw the cart, the harness and lamps of which were lying in the middle of the road. There was a mob of about 20 or 30 youths around the trap, but they all scampered away as soon as they caught site of the witness. The horse was not there, and apparently the defendant did not know where it was. Defendant was not drunk. Witness took charge of the harness and accompanied the defendant to Berwick station. Mrs Parker, wife of the previous witness gave similar evidence. Mrs Walker of Star Lane, Alfriston, denied that defendant was drunk. Defendant on oath denied being drunk. He admitted having something to drink at Alfriston, but he was quite capable of taking charge of a horse and cart. After a short consultation the Chairman said the Bench had decided that defendant was drunk and incapable of managing a horse and cart. They would therefore fine him £1 and costs. The money was paid."

○

In October 1874 many newspapers carried the story of a racehorse attacking Captain Charles Powell at Alfriston. The Captain was walking on his Deans Place farmland when he noticed the unaccompanied but saddled horse grazing alone. Realising the animal was trapped by the reins wrapped around his forelegs, he approached to help. The horse was quiet until he reached for the bridle then he snaked his head down and bit at the Captain's left side, lifted him off his feet, tore his clothing, dropped him and tried to kneel on him, repeating this several times. The prospect of being flattened by half a ton of angry horse is not a comfortable situation at all – Captain Powell was lucky to have survived. He may not have lived to tell the tale at all if James Gatland himself had not come galloping up in the nick of time and driven the offending horse back to the stables. The horse, owned by Arthur Harvey (and formerly the infamous 'Tichborne Claimaint' Arthur Orton) was in training at Wingrove.

○

Newspapers of 6th October 1922, reported a case of animal cruelty in Alfriston. The culprit was Rathfinny Farm incumbent, Everatt, who threatened the RSPCA inspector and PC Pullen with "You get off my farm and do some work. I will stick this fork in you." Undaunted the inspector carried out his duties and went into the field where three horses were harnessed to a farm wagon laden with corn. One, a bay mare, was lame in her forefeet and had no shoes on any hoof, the walls of her hooves were broken away, her feet were very hot and she kept trying to rest her forefeet in turn to ease the pain. The farm hand, Edmund Rose, said that she had come out of the stable very stiff that morning, there had been many stones in her hooves which he had picked out. Finding the mare unfit to work, the inspector and constable gave Everatt a warning and left. The next day they returned along with veterinary surgeon, Major Jackson, who quickly confirmed that the mare was totally lame, her hooves were worn right down to the sensitive quick, and it would take at least a month for them to regrow to a length that could take shoes. That same week Everatt was also brought to book over an aged, emaciated bay gelding, with diseased hind feet. The veterinarian said the gelding's days were numbered and work would exhaust him. John Henry Everatt paid for his neglect with a fine for his offence against the gelding and a month's prison with hard labour for his cruelty to the mare.

ᴜᕁᴜ

Mains drainage was very late coming to Alfriston, as Ron Levett wrote in his memoirs about his life growing up in Alfriston in the 1900s:

"There were no flush toilets in the village at that time ... Billie Bristow had the job of emptying the village's earth closets twice a week, using a tank on wheels pulled by a horse called 'Captain', who, when he was not working spent his days in the field opposite Alfriston Motors garage. Billie Bristow was reputed to grow the best vegetables in the village!"

Others remember Billie Bristow's cart being politely referred to as "sweet violets" and recall that it was still going about its service into the late 1950s.

Captain's field, which had also played host to many horses over the years, was located in the triangle formed by Deans Road, Kings Ride and Broadway – now it is full of houses.

"Captain's Field" – being enjoyed by local residents – Saffron Croft and Saffron House can be seen in the central background, along with barns behind the Star to the left.

Albert Wood, Alfriston's last butcher in a long family line, operated from Cross House in the village square behind which there was a stable for the horse used for deliveries. Right until his last couple of years, during Festival Week, Albert would hitch a horse to his ancient blue Wood & Sons butcher's cart, load up the back with 138lbs of his very special secret-recipe sausages, and go off to the Tye, where helpers Jean and Thelma would sell from the back of the cart. With the crowds forming a crocodile line tailing back over the Tye, the sausages sold out within twenty minutes.

Albert and his pony, Sally, were a popular spectacle on the Bank Holiday Monday of the Festival.

Albert Wood and pony Sally on the Tye for the annual
August Bank Holiday Festival.

Meanwhile, Winton Street had its equestrian activities as well.

Winton Street Farm operated as training stables in the mid-1900s, with a Mr R Tompsett residing at Winton House who in 1945 advertised for extra grazing for Thoroughbred mares.

In the late 50s/early 60s the house and yard were occupied by trainer Ken Eustace, who was described as a 'big fellow with a limp'. Local jockey Bunny Hicks would ride for him from time to time out on routine exercise and in races.

The original agricultural barns throughout the area of Winton Street were ultimately converted into residences one by one.

However, fortunately Winton Street stable complex remained just that and became a riding school in the ownership of the Wilkinson family. Later, in the 1970s the facility was owned by Brenda Eaton and run as a riding school and livery yard, and then later by Helen Clarke, who continued the riding school/livery yard business. The residence was a barn conversion in the yard.

Winton House has long been separated from the remainder of the barns, except for a short spell when Brenda Eaton re-united it with the main yard. It is separate again today.

Winton Street Farm had the benefit of the only indoor school in the area, which was a major boon to serious local riders who could hire the use of it for training their mounts for various types of competition. The arena is still there to this day, though now the facility is privately owned, with some of the original concrete block stabling also converted for human occupation, and new stabling created in a whole new timber barn.

The entrance to the Winton Street Farm stable yard

Helen Clarke working a horse in the indoor school

The now famous zoo park, Drusillas, when it was still in the ownership of the founding Ann family, had horse involvement as well. Growing up there, Michael Ann recalls it had a small livery yard/riding school of about twelve horses. An annual horse show and gymkhana would be organised in the surrounding fields and was well attended by competitors from miles around. The shows were open to all and enjoyed very much by spectators from the village.

Michael also ran a wedding carriage business for several years during the 1960s.

The Drusilla's Gymkhana underway with the Fancy Turnout class

Stanley, the wonderful grey Shire horse from Drusillas being led to the
Sussex Ox in 1978 by Tim Wickens with Fred Jordan and Lucy,
the Jack Russell terrier, on the beautiful farm wagon

Fred Holford and his brother came to Alfriston from Eastbourne.

Their cavalry/equestrian family owned riding stables in Eastbourne – at Ceylon Place and in Silverdale Road respectively for many years. But during Fred's time, Eastbourne grew increasingly urban and the popular beach rides became impossible, and the roads too risky, so he sought to move out to the country to carry on his equestrian business from the stabling at Paddock View, Alfriston.

Fred Holford on Mark – who became the first horse
purchased by the Eastbourne Constabulary

Later, he moved to The Poplars behind Alfriston Motors, where, for several decades, he ran his riding school from eleven loose boxes, taking his string of riders through the streets to the various downland tracks, and, on Sundays, along the Coach Road to The Cricketers Arms at Berwick, where an outdoor lunch was enjoyed by all, before returning to base. He was a familiar figure striding into the Star in his breeches, slapping his long boots with his crop, his spurs glinting. Fred was one of the village 'characters' whose presence is much missed.

His wife, Helen, continued with the riding school for a further twenty years but eventually called it a day in 1995. Their daughter took the remaining three horses – Timmy and his two companions – into her care at the barns at the King's Ride/ Broadway junction, and The Poplars was ultimately demolished and replaced with new housing between Alfriston Motors at the top of Star Lane and the existing Smugglers Close.

○

Together Bob and Julia Streeter took over Polegate Saddlery in 1983 which they ran together for over twenty-five years.

Julia inherited her love of horses from her father and had learned to ride at a riding school in Jevington, and later when the family moved to Alfriston she rode out regularly with Fred Holford in the village. She was 15 years old when she owned her first horse who she says was "definitely a Heinz 57 Irish job; he was 15.3hh and called Dougal."

Ex-jockey, Bob was immersed in horses from his first steps, starting with donkeys, moving on to ponies, and eventually to horses and being a jockey. Then he had a period as a re-enactor of historical battles, and worked in public presentations, on television and for films. Now retired, their facility in Alfriston is the forever home of several retired racehorses.

〇

In 1953 Len and Diane Savage acquired eighteen acres of the farm land opposite Deans Place, which was once part of the Wingrove racing scene, and there established their own facility known as Pleasant Rise. Len having been raised in Lewes, returned to Sussex when they left South Africa and found the land in Alfriston which they purchased with the intention of being self-sufficient. Initially there was no residence and while awaiting planning permission the couple and their children lived in a caravan on the land.

At the time of their purchase the land was used for raising bullocks, which once fat enough for market were walked through the village to River Lane and the slaughterhouse.

Len and Diane's son, Ray, talks of the pony, Susan, acquired for him from Milton Street. A Dartmoor/New Forest cross, dark bay and only 12.2hh, Susan took Ray on his daily trips to and from school. Susan led to the purchase of other horses for the family and pretty soon 'the old days' of grazing horses and riding up on to the Downs from France Bottom were lived out once again.

The Savage's family house was built in 1955 and in 1975 a further ninety or so acres were acquired, extending the Pleasant Rise holding up on to the top of the Downs. All the land had been given over for arable and the production of food in the war, but was reinstated to pasture later. The equestrian side developed into two yards, one that had once been the bullock yard was converted to stables, and the other is contained in a large open barn at the other end of the farm. Liveries and a riding school were the mainstay and, Ray points out, some of the people who had ridden there in their teen-days, have come back now with their own children. In the early 2000s it became known as the Alfriston Equestrian Centre which provided lessons and liveries, ran shows, and various educational equine courses. Interestingly, Ray confirms, it was the very first in the Cuckmere Valley to gain a riding school licence. Expanded into a tennis club with indoor and outdoor courts, and still in the family hands, the livery yards

continue, alongside extensive camping facilities in the approach to France Bottom. Perhaps, at dawn – the traditional morning exercise time for the racehorses – the echo of galloping hooves awakens the slumbering campers.

A section of France Bottom at Pleasant Rise – a tempting gallop indeed!

The village over the decades has been a regular meeting place for various hunts, including the Eastbourne Foxhounds and the Southdown and then the Southdown & Eridge.

Eastbourne Hunt in Market Square in 1911

The area to the west of the village known locally as The Uplands, was initially a horticultural holding with vast greenhouses, large orchard, and its own water cisterns and wells. The house had been built by 1908 and by 1950 it was home to the Goodridge family. The patriarch, Harry Goodridge, owned several harness horses and enjoyed driving them around locally and for shows. They were kept in his stable range at his home along with his impressive collection of antique carriages. He would maintain both horses and carriages with great care and was well respected for his ability and expertise.

In 1973 the family decided to sell, yet coincidentally the premises carried on the equine tradition, and became a small stud and showing yard, producing Arabian horses that were successful in the show rings, scooping international level prizes.

After their showing careers, two of those horses – King's Ride and King's Bucephalas – bred by and retained by the author, participated in the developing sport of Endurance (see Appendix 6).

King's Ride and King's Bucephalas at the Dunhill Marathon

Their many achievements culminated in the Dunhill Marathon of 1987 held at Belvoir Castle in Rutland. The marathon is a gruelling 26¼-mile race across natural countryside – a distance they covered in one hour and a few minutes.

These two equine village residents made history by being the only brothers to compete together, side by side, for the whole way, breasting the finishing line together. Yet another village-bred horse, from the same stud, was sold by the author to an Endurance rider who regularly undertook, and triumphed in, the even more exhausting 100-mile rides, including the internationally famous Golden Horseshoe on Exmoor.

◡

As if Alfriston's annals of horse history detailed earlier are not enough, there is also a very distinctive and unique record, an 'open equine secret', if you will. A serendipitous and most definitely diverse story as yet untold.

It began in the 1960s, when Fred Holford's Poplars Stables became the initial UK home of the very *first* Morgan Horse to be imported from the breed's homeland of the USA. Owned by the family of the now famous sculptress Angela Connor-Bulmer, the horse, named Melody, was shipped over and liveried in the village with Fred before eventually residing at the home of the Connor family. Later, based on this mare, Angela set up a stud at Monnington Court in Herefordshire, and nurtured the future of the Morgan Horse in Britain.

Albeit unintentionally, as it turned out, Melody kick-started a matchless tradition for the village for attracting yet more equine immigrants. All firsts. All trail-blazers.

Two decades after Melody and totally unconnected, the very first Tennessee Walking Horse to be imported to Britain, Pride of '76, strutted into Alfriston from the USA.

Pride with the author in the saddle on the Downs

Owned by Terry Cooke and Brenda Eaton of Winton Street Farm, this imposing liver-chestnut stallion, originally from Tennessee, swapped American show rings and high-stepping glamour, for a rather more laid back life-style in Alfriston.

After a year or so, he was moved to the author's private yard at Uplands where he joined another pioneering equine.

Meanwhile, realising a long-held ambition to return an American breed to its British genetic routes, the author had imported the very first five-gaited American Saddlebred[13] horse to reside in the UK.

From Kansas City, Rare Visions, as she was formally known – Scarlett to her friends – was a prime example of the remarkable abilities of this little-known breed. Being the first of the breed the quarantine farm on Long Island had encountered, she instantly generated transatlantic phone calls expressing their astonishment at her beauty, her exceptional manners and her amazing motion.

Rare Visions (living up to her name!) arrived into Stansted on 2nd May 1990 by Federal Express Jumbo Jet, just as the setting sun seeped through runway lighting and a fog of aviation fuel. Although FedEx was very accustomed to shipping racehorses globally, Rare Visions was the *first* American Saddlebred to be transported by them and the *first* to be handled by the importing agents, International Racehorse Transport. The ground staff responsible for unloading moved first to offload a consignment of paintings, leaving Scarlett and her travelling companion, a Thoroughbred, bereft in their shared specially designed in-flight stall. Outraged, the author apprehended the duty manager and insisted both horses be instantly offloaded and removed from the apron's traumatic environment.

"Oh no," came the jobs-worth reply. He indicated a stack of pallets, "We've gotta move these first. They're Her Majesty's paintings, you know."

---

[13] Full illustrated history and breed standard and can be found in the 'American Saddlebred' published by JA Allen as part of their popular Breeds Series.

Well, it was pointed out to him in no uncertain terms, "Paintings don't have feelings and they won't be stressed by their surroundings. The Queen would be outraged if she discovered horses had been traumatised for no reason!" He looked long and hard, obviously considering my possible royal 'connections', and then suddenly authorised the immediate offloading of both horses. Quite right too!

Untouched by jetlag, Scarlett bounded from her offloaded crate, amid gasps of amazement from the ground crew, and took those 'first steps for Saddlebred kind' on English ground. She travelled like a dream, disembarked at Uplands and marched with regal confidence into her new home yard as if parading in the show ring. What an eyeful. I admit to a mix of excitement and trepidation … I knew I had a huge learning curve ahead of me!

The author and Rare Visions at Essex County Show

But the village was merely a base, since these two American show-stoppers dazzled audiences with their distinctive displays and demonstrations, all over the country, taking the name of Alfriston with them!

Confronting total unawareness of the breeds, competing for 'air time' amidst already packed show schedules of 'known' competitors, getting 'the Americans' out there was a mission no less daunting than a 100-mile endurance race.

"Displaying a horse? What d'yuh do that for? American Saddlebreds? Never 'eard of 'em."

But one forward-thinking Show Secretary did agree it was a 'great idea' and just what she needed to keep the interest of audiences during the otherwise rather blank lunch time break between classes. Soon, more caught on and hot-hoof from Alfriston, these international go-getters were travelling the country thrilling audiences at venues as disparate as agricultural shows, equine festivals, horticultural shows, private events and indoor exhibitions. This start led to a trend for midday ring crowd-pleaser displays and entertainment with show secretaries booking entertainment of all equine kinds – dressage, jousting, Shires, etc. Now it is the norm.

Meanwhile, during the 1990s Scarlett and Pride showcased their specialist talents, displaying to music and with a commentary often done from the saddle – appearing all over the country at shows, riding club events, charity and private functions.

There is no doubt that the presence of Rare Visions and Pride of '76 in Alfriston, along with their national displays, generated many visitors to the village, including Americans, Europeans and

South Africans, most of whom enjoyed the hospitality and history, to be found in the hotels as well as adding, of course, to the local economy.

Over ensuing years, new enthusiasts were inspired to want their own Saddlebreds. Suitable horses for them have been located in the USA and imported directly to Uplands, where new owners were trained in how to ride and produce these specialist animals, ultimately to take their place in a unique-in-the-world dedicated British Display Team of American Saddlebreds.

Part of the Display Team posing with the Earl of Carnarvon at Highclere Castle
Left to right: Robin Neal on Wildest Heart, Will's Gazette, the Earl, Cheryl Lutring, Jane Green in the sulky and Holly Neal on Harlem Bay.

This unique in the world team appeared all around the country from The Earl of Carnarvon's Highclere Castle (of Tutankhamun and Downton Abbey fame) in Berkshire to the National Equestrian Centre at Stoneleigh in Warwickshire, Arena

UK in Leicestershire, county shows from Lincolnshire to Wiltshire, the exclusive Polo grounds of Cowdray Park in Sussex, from crowds of thousands cramming the Surrey County Showground to the hallowed surface of London's Rotten Row – and at many other events for schools, charities and equestrian clubs. Several displays were also organised at Uplands exclusively for Alfriston residents.

One of the horses and team member, based at Uplands – Will's Gazette and owner Jane Green – made the very first driven appearance in Britain of an American Saddlebred in Fine Harness, competing at the Royal Windsor Horse Show and parading in front of HM The Queen.

In addition the team also were presenting a different style of riding/driving and new style of turnout and presentation, known in the USA as 'saddle-seat'.

Lord Gage and Lord Healey presenting Will's Gazette
with his commemorative rosette on his retirement from public life.
Driven to an American show sulky by his owner, Jane A Green.

Five gaited
Saddlebred team
member Wildest
Heart ridden
by owner Robin Neal

To summarise this extraordinary triple piece of equine history: the first Morgan horse, the first Tennessee Walking Horse and the first Five-Gaited American Saddlebred to be imported from USA to UK, all came to reside first in Alfriston village!

One thing is certain: Alfriston has a long, remarkable, very varied and unique horse history ... a heritage of which to be particularly proud.

ᑌᑌᑌ

APPENDICES

Alfriston and Litlington share their very own 'white horse' carved in the chalk on the eastern flank of High & Over.

The current horse is a replacement for one carved to commemorate Queen Victoria's coronation. Carved by moonlight in 1924 by a local trio of young men as a prank, it is now maintained by the National Trust.

APPENDIX 1

Initially horseracing occurred informally and was staged on any stretch of available land. Rules were instituted and applied as the organisers saw fit and would vary from racecourse to racecourse as conditions demanded. Races consisted mainly of 'matches' between the personal mounts of the contenders – "I'll wager my nag can beat yours."

However, due to public enthusiasm racing escalated and by 1685 Royal Plates were offered which were run under specific rules, at approved venues, required entry fees, offered prizes and provided categories open to anyone who thought his horse good enough. Rules covered distances, heats, size of horse, type of horse, weight of jockey, maiden racers, etc.

In Queen Anne's reign (1702-1714) the Plate events even provided for three-heat races for children under 6 years with £100 to the winner.

Government became concerned by the burgeoning popularity of the sport and in 1740 saw fit to issue an Act of Parliament that sought to prevent the excessive increase in horse races. Basically it failed and racing grew and grew. However, it was acknowledged that some sort of consistent ruling needed to be in place. The Jockey Club was formed in 1750 with the idea of marshalling the sport into a set standard with strict rules and conditions. Gradually it reduced Royal influence over the Sport of Kings.

APPENDIX 2

In the words of the Imperial War Museum:

> "In the first year of war (WW1) the countryside was emptied of shire horses and riding ponies, a heart-breaking prospect for farming families who saw their favourite and most beloved horses requisitioned by the government. … The loss of horse life greatly exceeded the loss of human life in the terrible battles of the Somme and Passchendaele."

Not only were horse lives lost wholesale, but the suffering, terror, and sheer trauma of the whole experience meant he had to endure, as General Seely said of his horse: "… everything most hateful to him – violent noise, the bursting of great shells and bright flashes at night, when the white light of bursting shells must have caused violent pain to such sensitive eyes as horses possess. Above all, the smell of blood, terrifying to every horse. Many people do not realise how acute is his sense of smell, but most will have read his terror when he smells blood. The sombre close of the Battle of the Somme was cruel to horses no less than men," said General Seely. "…Often these poor beasts would sink deep into the mud and in spite of all their struggles, they could not extricate themselves, and died where they fell."

The increasing difficulty of replacing horses was so critical by 1917 that some troops were told that the loss of a horse was of greater tactical concern than the loss of a human soldier.

Back home, the trauma inflicted on decent humans and their children by the arrival of the Remount Service teams to take their equine partners away for war would have been immeasurable.

It's hard to imagine words more chilling than "your horse belongs to the Army now".

There were eight Collecting Stations in Sussex – the one for the Alfriston area being at Lewes cattle market, where there was sufficient space for 100 horses at a time.

And there was little comfort from the conclusion of the War either, because those that survived the hell of the battlefield and manoeuvres, were abandoned to their miserable fate when the armies returned home. The lucky ones, if that can be said, were actually shot by the soldiers who worked with them so they would be spared the future of torment that faced them.

Some returned home to fanfare and comfort … but they were just a few out of the nine million that died in World War One.

> "...and there are wounded horses ..,
> the undecorated, unnamed heroes of the battle
> who for a hundred, two hundred miles have
> hauled this artillery, now dead and
> drowning in the swamp."
> *Alexander Solzhenitsyn,* 1914

APPENDIX 3

1891   stable lads Harry King, Harry Marchant, James Jacob and Jesse Baker lodged on the west side of the High Street.

James Parr, coachman and groom, lived on the east side of the High Street.

Various grooms and coachmen took care of the horses of the families in the big houses of the village, and often lodged with them or nearby. For example, Saddlers House in the High Street had a stable at the back; and both Tuckvar and Cross House had stables and coach houses at the rear.

The Star, George and Market Cross all had facilities for horses. The Market Cross (aka The Smugglers) stabled the pack horses and mounts of the 'Alfriston Gang' and had extra doors to aid speedy escape for the smugglers!

George A Butchers, 25-year old steeplechase jockey and groom, with his family, lived in the High Street. Butchers was a successful jockey, who moved to Lewes (Pelham Arms Stables) where he also trained racehorses. (For more on the Butchers family see *Lewes Racecourse | A Legacy Lost?*)

Blacksmith Edmund Olive and blacksmith/farrier William Turner lived in Brickkiln Cottages.

Frederick Woolgar's son Harvey was a hack driver and groom and the other son, William, was a blacksmith alongside his father at the Forge at Sloe Field.

APPENDIX 4

According to the records the number of horses the whole of East Sussex in 1924 was 12,439. This included 10,019 working in agriculture and 2,420 'others' – presumably this means riding horses and maybe racehorses.

Today county figures are not available, but Alfriston itself is home to approximately sixty horses of all types and breeds, including retired racehorses, rescue ponies and cobs, driving ponies, pleasure horses for hacking out and competition, youngsters whose career trails are yet to be defined, pensioners living out their allotted span on downland pasture, all kept in private facilities or in the one remaining livery yard at Pleasant Rise.

APPENDIX 5

From 1894 until at least 1997 the Alfriston Plate race was run annually at Brighton featuring as the first race of the August meeting. In addition, the Alfriston 'Chase was run at Newbury from approximately 1910 to 1938. In 1920 Bottomley's horse Macmerry (trained by Batho) was fancied to win the Alfriston 'Chase but was beaten by a neck by Memento.

Every effort has been made to identify the instigator of these races and hence the reason for the name. Brighton Racecourse does have some races named after the villages close by to it, but this is hardly a motive for Newbury. So far nothing has been turned up to explain the naming of these races.

APPENDIX 6

The sport of Equine Endurance involves riding across country on a specific course for set mileages – 25 miles, 40 miles, 50 miles or 100 miles. The courses are challenging and are not prepared in any way, gates must be opened and closed, rivers forded, steep hills climbed or slithered down, etc. Horses (and riders) must be extremely fit. Health checks are rigorous, and heart rates of horses are taken at the beginning and again at the end when they must be within the parameters set – just three or four beats per minute difference. On longer rides there are also veterinary gates *en route* to check heart rates at that time too. Any horse with a heart rate higher than required is eliminated. Unlike the Marathons, Endurance is not a race against other contenders but against yourself and the terrain. Awards are not 1st, 2nd, 3rd etc. but Grade 1 and Grade 2. Any number of entries achieving the criteria may be awarded Grade 1 or 2. This makes it a very sociable and enjoyable sport, though most of the route is often traversed alone.

Feeding and training a horse to be fit enough to stand the pace – 25 miles should normally be covered in 1¼ hours at most – is quite exacting and requires daily training. The venues for Endurance Rides can be anywhere in the country, but a very popular annual one is right here on the South Downs. The 25-mile level usually starts in Firle Park, comes along from Bo Peep, down the military road to Sanctuary and on over Longbridge to Friston Forest and Jevington, returning down Peachey's, up Winton Street, and back to Firle along the Coach Road.

APPENDIX 7

Although shown as being in Alfriston, in the 1920s the elusive David Dale's stables were at Tide Mills (south of Bishopstone) where he could accommodate at least eight horses. Their healing and rehabilitation, included exercise on the sands and in the sea – just meters away – washing the salt and sand off their legs afterwards in the purpose-built clean water dip. Swimming exercise was often undertaken by leading the horse from a rowing boat.

All that remains now are ruined outer walls, traces of the loose boxes – each approximately 10' x 10', one with a ruined but extant manger, the others with floor markings indicating where the mangers were.

Above left: David Dale riding in the surf

Above right: horse being allowed a relaxing roll in the sand

Left: the wash off dip today

Acknowledgements

The input of so many is much appreciated. These include:

Jane Clarke, Aintree Museum Curator and historian, for her interest and input regarding Wild Man From Borneo.

Richard Hayward for generously allowing access to his family's racing documents and vast collection of photographs.

www.gravelroots.net

The Cox Racing Library
British Horseracing Authority
National Horse Racing Museum, Newmarket
Illustrated Sporting & Dramatic News, multiple editions
Bell's Life in London & Sporting Chronicle, Aug 1868
Kelly's Directory – multiple years
National Archives, Kew
British Newspapers Archive
East Sussex Record Office

J & J Dudeney, Sussex Yeomanry	Mrs S Prior
Lesley Goodchild	Ian Thomson
John Harmer	Barry Norman
Helen Holford	Mark Driver
Barbara Hutchinson	Ray Savage
Karen Ray-Gain, Bede's School	Bunny Hicks
Bob Streeter	Stephen Carr
Alan Kirk	John Lower
Tony Sawden	Gregory Ade
Captain & Mrs Palmer	Richard Wood
June Doyle	Helen Clarke

Bibliography

Alfriston Past & Present, W H Johnson, 1998

Alfriston: The Story of a Downland Village, Alfred Cecil Piper, 1970

Alfriston Today & Yesterday, Edna and Mac McCarthy, 1982

All The Kings' Horses, Amanda Murray, 2003

Bottomley's Book, Horatio Bottomley, 1909

Child of the Twenties, Frances Donaldson

Cuckmere, The, Edna & Mac Mccarthy, 1981

Dead & Buried in Sussex, David Arscott, reprint 2007

Early Victorian Alfriston, W H Johnson, 1993

History of Alfriston, Florence Pagden, 1906 (third edition)

Horatio Bottomley, Julian Symons, 2001

Wingrove & The Churchill Connection, June Goodfield &
Peter Robinson, 2010

The Rise & Fall of Horatio Bottomley, Alan Hyman, 1972

Racing Illustrated, March 1896

Illustrated Sporting & Dramatic News, multiple editions 1800-1900

Illustrations from the past are rarities and therefore for the sake of the record the
priority in their selection has been their information-value and relevance rather than
reproductive quality.

Previous publications by Cheryl R Lutring

The Allen Guides to Horse Breeds: American Saddlebred (2005)
"A tremendous outreach work of international value."
American Saddlebred Horse Association, Kentucky

Monumental Equus: Honouring the Horse (2010)
"Changed my view about horses – amazing heart-warming stuff."
R Hart

"ME has pride of place on my coffee table, guests love to dip in and we are all amazed by the wonderful horses featured."
Patricia Crane, internationally renowned equine sculptress, USA

War Horse … Biopics (2011)
"The individual stories of horses in war had never occurred to me – so poignant. An eye-opener in many ways."
R H Martin

Lewes Racecourse │A Legacy Lost? (2013; 2nd edition 2014)
"This book is the model for a racecourse history. ... Lewes Racecourse is brought alive by the personalities that have been involved. Congratulations." Tim Cox, The Cox Racing Library

"… in these pages you will find many fascinating anecdotes about the myriad cast of personalities, both human and equine, with connections to the town … cannot help but derive knowledge and enjoyment from this beautifully researched volume."
The Lord Rathcreedan, Chair, Stewarding Panel, British Horseracing Authority

Sapley, Personal Reflections of A Hampshire Family Farm (2014)
"A unique approach to local and personal history. A very readable and illuminating book."
J. Atkinson

In addition she writes on horses in history for magazines around the world, including the UK's *Horse & Hound* and America's oldest and largest monthly equine publication, *Saddle & Bridle*.

She has received international awards and recognition for her work in enhancing public understanding of the USA's national breed, the American Saddlebred, and the role of horses throughout the development humankind. In particular in 2007 she received the only International Award issued by the Saddlebred governing body in Kentucky, USA, for her international outreach – her acceptance speech at the Annual Awards Ball at Keeneland Racecourse receiving the first ever standing ovation from the audience of oil, gold, diamond and publishing magnates.

American Saddlebred stallion Attache's Leading Admiral at Uplands

Short Glossary of horse terms

Cab: a horse drawn vehicle for public hire, diminutive of 'cabriolet' – a small two-seater two-wheeled carriage with a folding hood.

Fly: light one-horse covered carriage let out for hire.

Trap: light two wheeled carriage drawn by one horse or pony, usually for private use.

Thoroughbred: a horse developed in the 17th century for its refinement and speed, used in horse racing.

Cob: a small stocky strong horse that is between being a horse or a pony. Enjoys a reputation for reliability, stamina and general usefulness.

Horse: an equine standing at over 14.2 hands high (a hand being 4 inches). Horses are measured from the ground to the top of their withers (the highest point at the base of the neck).

Pony: a small equine of under 14.2 hands high (a hand being 4 inches) most suitable for pulling small carts, as riding animals for children, and as a pack animal.

Stud: refers directly to an entire male horse otherwise known as a stallion; or can mean the premises where horses are bred.

Index

uUu

In the event of major omissions or errors,
please let us know, as amendments can be made
in future editions.